EIGHTH NOTE  PUBLICATIONS

Barricade

Ryan Meeboer

T0054386

Barricade is a fun, high energy piece that gives beginning students the opportunity to learn to play with rhythmic precision and demonstrate their abilities as performers.

To start, the tempo marking 'With Aggression' identifies that the piece is to be played with assertiveness throughout. This means that each of the notes are to be played with an accented feel, even though they are not all marked as such. Along with this, the piece also opens with strong dynamics. Be sure that students begin with the appropriate dynamic so the piece opens with good tone quality and good dynamic contrast can be used throughout the rest of the piece.

The main melody is introduced at measure 10 with block harmonies accompanying it. Make sure the melodic material is prominent over these harmonies, as some performers may become excited and over play their material.

In the contrasting section at measure 26, make sure the slurs are played smoothly without performers clipping the note at the end of the slur. The section will build naturally by the addition of instruments at measure 30, so make sure players do not create their own dynamic increase until measure 32.

Measures 42 through 49 is another great opportunity to work on dynamic contrast with the gradual increase of volume from the beginning of the section to the end. This also leads into measure 50 where the lower sections get the opportunity to play some melodic material.

As the piece comes to a close, make sure the energy level stays high, but the final notes are not over blown and the piece can end with the same tone quality as it began.

Ryan Meeboer is a music educator, who obtained his degree through the Ontario Institute for Studies in Education at the University of Toronto. As a composer, he has written and arranged many pieces for concert band, jazz band, and small ensembles. His young band piece, *Last Voyage of the Queen Anne's Revenge*, has been well received by performers, educators, and audiences, and his pieces are starting to be found on festival and contest lists. As a performer, he has had experience in several groups, including concert and stage bands, chamber choir, vocal jazz ensemble, acoustic duets, and the Hamilton based swing group, "The Main Swing Connection".

Ryan began studying music at the age of seven through private guitar lessons. During his years in elementary and secondary school, he gained experience in several families of instruments. Focusing on music education and theory (including composition and orchestration), he attended McMaster University to achieve his honours degree in music. Ryan is currently a teacher for the Halton District School Board in Ontario, where he continues to compose and arrange.

*Please contact the composer if you require any further information about this piece
or his availability for commissioning new works and appearances.*

ryan.meeboer@enpmusic.com

ISBN: 9781771578653
CATALOG NUMBER: BQ222542
COST: $15.00
DURATION: 1:45
DIFFICULTY RATING: Easy
Brass Quintet

www.enpmusic.com

BARRICADE

Ryan Meeboer

BARRICADE pg. 2

BARRICADE

B♭ Trumpet 1

Ryan Meeboer

BARRICADE pg. 2

Bb Trumpet 2

BARRICADE

Ryan Meeboer

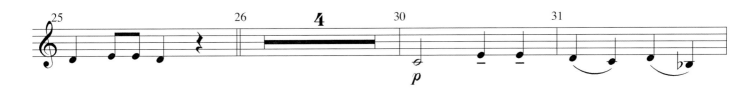

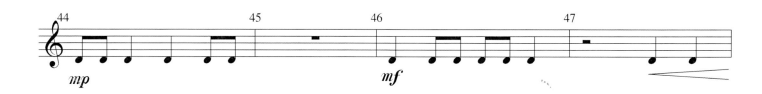

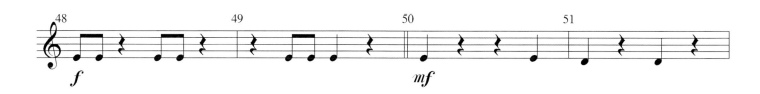

BARRICADE pg. 2

F Horn

BARRICADE

Ryan Meeboer

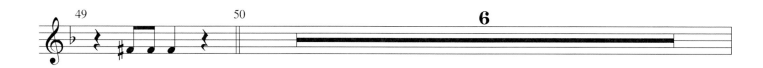

BARRICADE pg. 2

Trombone

BARRICADE

Ryan Meeboer

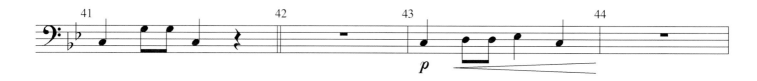

BARRICADE pg. 2

Tuba

BARRICADE

Ryan Meeboer

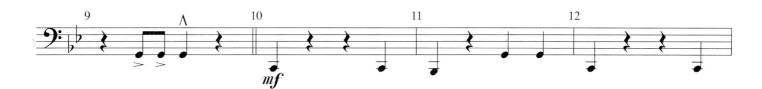

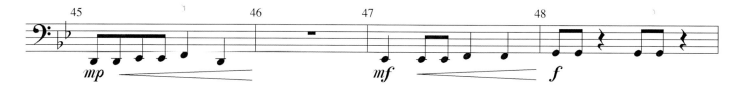

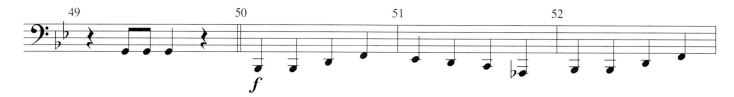

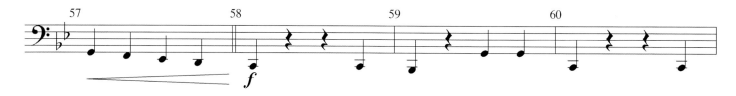

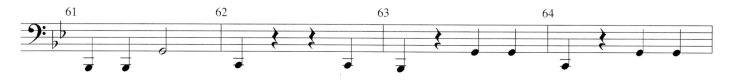

BARRICADE pg. 2